TO SET PROMETHEUS FREE

A. C. Grayling

TO SET PROMETHEUS FREE

Essays on Religion, Reason and Humanity

OBERON BOOKS

LONDON

First published in 2009 by Oberon Books Ltd

521 Caledonian Road, London N7 9RH

Tel: 020 7607 3637 / Fax: 020 7607 3629

e-mail: info@oberonbooks.com

www.oberonbooks.com

ISBN: 978-1-84002-962-8

Printed in Great Britain by CPI Antony Rowe, Chippenham

Contents

Preface

IN 2007 I published a short book called *Against All Gods: Six Polemics Against Religion and an Essay on Kindness*. The essays in that book were deliberately short and robustly expressed; they were polemical contributions to the debate – quarrel would be a better word – about religion galvanised by the attack on the World Trade Center's twin towers in New York and the Pentagon in Washington, carried out on 11 September 2001 by a group of men expressly in the name of their religion, Islam, which they claimed to provide justification for the act. They were celebrated by many in the Islamic world for what they did. Those atrocities – the indiscriminate mass murder of several thousand people going about their daily lives – were neither the cause nor the beginning of the quarrel, but they kicked it into a new and very much higher gear; and people who beforehand had kept silent about, or anyway muted in, their critical opinion of religion and its effect on the world, now felt impelled to speak out, and to do so without mincing words.

The essays in *Against All Gods* are examples of that new mood, though I had been writing for years beforehand in much the same critical vein about the need for a greater secularism. I stand by everything said in *Against All Gods*, and even by its tone: frank speaking about religion is needful now, because quieter methods of abating its negative influence have manifestly failed. Frank speaking is not the same thing as burning at the stake, which is what votaries of religion used to do to their critics in earlier times: Richard Dawkins, Christopher Hitchens and Sam Harris might tongue-lash the faithful, but if they had lived a few centuries ago and ventured the same opinions, they would have received far more than hard words in return. It is a thought that often recurs when apologists of religion complain that the views of the so-called 'new atheists', or the manner of their statement, have offended them; I reflect that if the clock were turned back enough, some of these same folk might be gathering faggots for kindling even as they complained. And alas, that is what still happens in parts of the world where the grip of religion remains oppressive and too often dangerous to the lives and well-being of many.

The brevity of the essays in *Against All Gods* served a purpose. Correspondents and others have asked for a fuller and more detailed statement of the case against religion: I offer it in the essays collected here.

My thanks go to the editors of the books and journals in which some of these essays first appeared, and to the work and personal communications of friends and colleagues in the community of those working in defence of a rational and evidence-based view of the world: Richard Dawkins, Christopher Hitchens, Sam Harris and the Reason Project, Roger Bingham and the Beyond Belief series, Daniel Dennett, Harry Kroto, Lawrence Krauss, Jerry Coyne, P. Z. Myers, Steven Pinker, and others.

The essays which had their origin elsewhere are 'Why I do not subscribe to religious beliefs' and 'Why Bertrand Russell was not religious'. The ancestor of the first was commissioned by Russell Blackford and Udo Schüklenk for their excellent and compelling volume *50 Voices of Disbelief* (Wiley Blackwell 2009) and the second was commissioned by Nick Trakakis and Graham Oppy for the fifth volume of their monumental *History of the Philosophy of Religion* (Oxford University Press 2009). 'Scientists confront Intelligent Design and Creationism' and 'The war of the books' were responses to publications, and the latter had multiple origins in *New Humanist* magazine.

I

Where are we in history?

WHERE ARE WE in human history? Are we close to the end of mankind's story, either because we are in the process of making our world uninhabitable, or because the wars and conflicts that perennially wrack us will escalate to a catastrophe? Or are we at the beginning of history, just starting to have the means – through technology and its promise for education, health, communication, global co-operation – which will help us become wise enough at last to live in peace, so that we can devote our pooled energies and resources wholly to progressive endeavours?

The answer to both questions is Yes – and there is no contradiction in saying so. We might be close to the end of humanity's history because of environmental damage or because conflict could get out of hand – or more likely both, because each makes the other worse. But if we survive climate change and a rash of nuclear wars, we will find that we are still at an early stage of human development, an immature stage, barely adolescent, only just at the beginning of scientific understanding of the world, still wedded to infantile beliefs and practices that are holding us back and causing or exacerbating the harms that threaten our existence.

The chief of these divisive, regressive obstacles is superstition, not least in its organised form as religion. It is not possible to underestimate the drag on human history that religion represents, standing in the way of progress towards individual liberation, the gathering and application of scientific knowledge, the development of open and pluralistic societies, and the adoption of a humane morality which is tolerant, generous, inclusive and just, and in which it is the fact of being human rather than the ethnicity, gender or sexuality of individuals that determines how they treat each other.

Of course religion is not the only problem confronting mankind – economic and other forms of injustice loom large among those problems too – but it is a very major one, and in recent years it has returned to being more open and active in its resistance to the modern world. We see creationists in America opposing science and science education, Anglicans refusing to countenance gay relationships, Catholics opposing important medical research, ultra-orthodox Jews provocatively building settlements on Palestinian land, Hindus beating Muslims to death, fundamentalist Muslims repressing women, reacting with infantile violence to criticism of Islam's sacred texts and prophets, and in some of its extremer reaches encouraging indiscriminate mass murder through terrorism. This just skims the surface of an utterly unacceptable situation, in which large portions of mankind remain in some degree of thrall to myths dating from an ignorant and illiterate past.

A tide has turned, though, in attitudes about religion on the part of those who do not share its sentiments. Until the end of the twentieth century there was an elephant-in-the-room attitude towards religion. People without religion would, by and large, maintain a polite silence when confronted with someone who avowed a faith, though it was usually only those among the latter who lacked taste or sufficient social sense who would speak about their religious commitments at what we would then have thought inappropriate moments, such as a dinner party or in a meeting at work. The only public avowals of religion by otherwise normal-seeming people were made by American politicians seeking election, with sometimes comic results. Democratic candidate Howard Dean from New England, prompted by his minders to make friendly noises towards religion for the sake of possible electors in the Bible Belt of his country, got someone to ask him to nominate his favourite book of the New Testament (*New* Testament, note); he answered, 'The Book of Job'. No one minded; he had made a vaguely Biblical noise, and that was enough.

But everything changed on an identifiable date. The atrocity now universally known as '9/11' – the attack by suicidal Islamic fanatics flying hijacked aircraft into the twin towers of New York's World Trade Center and the Pentagon in Washington – changed all that. Suddenly people who had kept a polite silence when confronted with someone whose beliefs are premised on the superstitions of illiterate goatherds living over two thousand years ago, were no longer prepared to stay either silent or polite. The whole history of religion's oppressions, repressions and oppositions to progress, its promotion of lunatic and murderous certainties, its capacity to justify huge wrong, came shudderingly back into focus. The elephant is crashing about in the room, trampling people to death, and politely ignoring it is no longer an option.

Religion's critics now speak bluntly of what they really think about it – a bluntness that makes the faithful protest in indignation: but the faithful forget that wherever and whenever they have the upper hand, they do not restrict themselves to blunt speech in opposing those who oppose them, but take blunt action: burning people at the stake, stretching them on the rack, hanging them as they do in today's Iran, stoning them as they do in today's Saudi Arabia, cutting off their heads as they do in the Taliban-controlled parts of today's Afghanistan.

Religion's apologists protest that this is a one-sided caricature of religion only: they insist that we remember charity, art, plainsong, soaring cathedrals, the comforts provided by faith, the spiritual dimensions of life. These things are deliberately neglected by our critics, say the religionists, who give a deliberately and indeed maliciously skewed portrait of religion as a result.

To which I reply: the kind acts of charity, the making of beautiful art, the giving of comfort, the heightened numinous sense of the universe's oneness and majesty, are not the monopoly of religious people. There are many non-religious people who are charitable, comforting, makers and enjoyers of art, and deeply moved by the universe. They are not people who think that these things can only be explained in terms of the existence of supernatural agencies, who at the same time, not untypically, threaten eternal torments to non-believers and gays, and who prompt their faithful to kill and die for what goatherds long ago superstitiously believed. No, the positive things that defenders of religion claim for religion are not the monopoly of religion; but killing people for alleged blasphemy and heresy, for going after false gods, for desecrating such fetishes as holy texts or icons or the memory of prophets, for not wearing a beard or eating meat on Fridays or being a woman who dares think or choose for herself – these crimes are committed only with the special sanction of religion; they are marks of the mental pathology that is religious faith.

One major task in reducing the conflict and regressiveness in our world, therefore, is to abate the nuisance of religion. So let me be clear what I mean by this, as follows.

Three separable but naturally connected debates are involved here. There is a metaphysical debate about what the universe contains. There is a debate about the place of religious organisations and movements in society. And there is a debate about the basis and nature of ethics. The first concerns the quarrel between theists and atheists. The second concerns secularism and the degree to which religion should have a footprint in the public square. The third concerns the claim by theists that there can be no morality unless there is an invisible police force in the sky that will give you a bad time after death if you sin, and reward you if you behave as your religion instructs you. Humanism is the family of non-religious alternatives to such an ethics.

In the essays to follow I discuss the first and third – the metaphysical and the ethical – debates. Here a few remarks will suffice on the secularism question.

In any liberal democratic society, people must be free to think and believe what they like, provided they do no harm to others. The problem is, religion too frequently does harm. And one main reason why it is able to do so is because of the inflated place it has in the public sphere. Take Britain as an egregious example: the Anglican version of Christianity is the established religion of the state. Twenty-six bishops are entitled to sit in the House of Lords, there to vote on legislation affecting the whole country; a number of retired bishops and archbishops are given life peerages to swell their ranks. Public tax money goes to funding faith-based schools, thus ghettoising children into separate religious communities – an experiment that violently and tragically failed in Northern Ireland, but despite that is being expanded in mainland Britain. The publicly-funded broadcasting service, the BBC, has a dedicated 'Religion and Ethics Broadcasting Unit' which puts out several religious programmes every day of the week, every week of the year. And all this take place against this background: that the number of regular weekly attenders at churches, mosques, temples and synagogues totals less than 10 per cent of the country's population. This is a stark example of the grossly over-amplified voice, the massively over-inflated, publicly-subsidised presence of religion in the public square. And of course the United Kingdom is far from alone in the world in this respect.

The solution? Religious organisations and movements should be seen, and should see themselves, for what they are: self-constituted special-interest groups, civil society organisations of the same stamp as political parties, trades unions, lobbying groups and NGOs. They have every right to exist and to have their say, but no greater right than any other self-constituted civil society group. These other groups are not given public money, tax-exempt status, their own broadcast programmes, seats in Parliament, and tax dollars to run schools to proselytise the young into their particular political, trades union or stamp-collecting way of thinking. The religions have exploited their historical position to gain a vast advantage over other such organisations. They use it to keep their reactionary views tangled around the feet of science, society and progress; in most of the world they use it subjugate women, murder those who do not agree with their beliefs or observe their practices, justify wars, and generally, too often, make themselves a cancer in the body of humanity.

Apart from relegating religious groups to ordinary civil society organisations by removing the various and many privileges that keep a megaphone to their mouths out of all proportion to their merits or numbers, there is the difficult question of whether, if they wish to brainwash their small children into their beliefs, they should be allowed to do so, even at their own expense. Liberal principles and acceptance of the view that parents have a right to determine their children's faith and education together point in the direction of accepting this. Well: I wonder. Does society have a duty to protect the young from proselytisation? Think of a row of chubby little babies, each with a label around its neck, one label saying 'Democrat', the next 'Communist', the next 'Republican' – would we not be outraged at the implication? But so with religion: no one is born a Muslim, a Hindu or a Christian; a considerable effort has to be applied to making them so. To become committed devotees of the faith that their parents and communities wish them to be, they have to be told many falsehoods, stuffed with many fantasies and absurdities, and rendered incapable of thinking for themselves sufficiently to challenge the falsehoods and fantasies in question.

Indeed the single largest factor that keeps the antique faiths of the world in existence is the proselytisation of the young. While we think as we do about what is acceptable in the way of parents' rights over children, and what children can therefore be made to believe while they are intellectually defenceless in their earliest years, we need the robust and vociferous counterblast of arguments against religion on all three fronts of metaphysics, secularism and ethics, in the hope of rescuing as many as possible from the prison-house of religious belief, and liberating them into the sunlit uplands of free thinking, open minds, a vigorous sense of personal responsibility for their values and actions, a clear-eyed vision of the world, and an interest in participating in the great adventure of finding out more about it.

So let us return to the question of where we are in history. Palaeoanthropologists hypothesise that when the ancestors of modern humans left Africa, they did so in small numbers making a perilous journey through a bottleneck: perhaps the isthmus of land through which the Suez Canal now runs, or perhaps the short passage across the Bab el-Mandeb at the southernmost point of the Red Sea. Like their distant forebears, today's human beings are again passing through a perilous bottleneck, trying to navigate the environmental and ideological dangers that threaten to extinguish humankind before it can escape into the broad fertile plains of possibility that lie beyond them.

I see human history thus: for many tens of thousands of years our ancestors struggled with the challenge of survival, in small numbers, with one weapon at their disposal – not claws or sabre-teeth or venomous stings, but intelligence and eventually its great potentiator, language. In those indeterminate epochs, fifty to a hundred thousand years ago and more, our ancestors employed stories about their environment – about the animals, the weather, the rivers, the landscape, very much as Australia's aboriginals still do – which helped them to relate to it, to encapsulate their understanding of it, and to pass that understanding on to their inheritors. Despite the tools, burial remains and cave art of these ancestors, together with the residual examples of such culture in the present, we can only surmise what their theories of the world were like. But it

might be reasonable to assume that they constituted a kind of proto-science, a set of explanations
probably couched in anthropomorphic or animist
terms. Thus, perhaps, they thought that thunder is
caused by a giant being walking on the clouds, that
lightning is a spear it threw down to earth; a river
flooded because an agency within it was angry; the
beings who control the rain can be supplicated for
help; and so on. This is not supernaturalism, but a
form of naturalism; it explains nature in the most
obvious way, by imputing to it the same intention-
ality and agency as humans themselves possess. But
as practical knowledge and understanding of nature
increased, these agencies were thought of in more
and more remote terms – they were shifted off to
mountain tops, into the sun, into the sky, finally
beyond space and time itself. They became supernatural, shrouded in mystery, interpreted by special-
ised priesthoods who thereby exercised control and
influence over society, and who were therefore useful
to the temporal powers, who encouraged, protected
and abetted the priests in their influence. And that is
why the religions remain potent forces in the world
today, fundamentally because of the unholy alliance
they forged with those who saw their usefulness in
keeping the majority in line.

The first Enlightenment that we know of in human history occurred in the classical epoch of ancient Greece. In very summary outline, the science and philosophy of classical antiquity was an enlightenment in just the same way as the eighteenth century Enlightenment, for it sought to apply reason, observation and scientific method to the quest for an understanding of the world and human society without reliance on supernaturalistic explanations. The achievements of the classical world, all its deficits acknowledged, are astonishing across the range from literature to engineering, from architecture to government, from quality of life to empire. The irruption into the classical world of the oriental superstition of Christianity interrupted the course of progress for a thousand years – the thousand years between the basilica of Maxentius in Rome and Brunelleschi's dome for Florence's cathedral, for until the latter was achieved, no one knew how to repeat the architectural and engineering feat of the basilica. That is merely a marker of what was lost when religion became the main issue, destroying a civilisation by its schisms, heresies, its divisions, internal weakness, its focus not on the human good in this life but a suppositious utopia in a posthumous existence. Only in Byzantium did the strength of the classical inheritance survive long enough – but by no means completely – under the weight imposed on it by Christianity for some of the lineaments of that civilisation to survive. It took another equally destructive religion to erase it completely.

Let us put a little flesh on the bones of the foregoing claim, by making two points: one about what classical civilisation promised, and one about the submersion of Western mankind in a long dark age because of the hegemony of Christianity (this latter woeful tale is well told, correct in all outline, by Gibbon's *Decline and Fall*).

The first point is made by the example of Thales of Miletus, who lived about 600 BCE and who was regarded by Aristotle as the first in the great tradition of philosophy in classical antiquity. He asked himself a question that many must have asked before, namely 'What explains the world? What is its origin, what is it made of ultimately? What is its *arché*, its principle?' It is his answer that makes him the first of the 'physicists', as the early philosophers were known. He did not reach for myths or supernatural explanations, for doing this is not an explanation but merely pushes the mystery back into another and even more obscure mystery (that is what 'there is a god who created the world' uselessly does). Instead he observed, and reasoned. He concluded that the ultimate stuff of which the world is made is water. Water is ubiquitous; it is in the sea, the rivers, the veins of men, the sap of trees, and it falls from the sky – which shows that the sky itself is water. Water is necessary to life; nothing survives without it. It alone among the substances known to Thales could take all three forms of solid, liquid and gas: solid when it froze, liquid in its normal state, gas when it boiled away in steam or rose in vapour. And from it, said Thales, comes earth, as the silt of the Nile shows.

Thales was of course wrong, but it is not the answer itself so much as the manner of its formulation which sets him apart, and likewise the whole tradition that came after him – a tradition in which Pythagoras saw that number describes the basis of reality and that the earth is spherical, in which Democritus and Leucippus formulated the atomic hypothesis, in which Xenophanes understood the implications of finding sea shells on mountain tops, in which Anaximander hypothesised the evolution of life forms from the sea, in which Alcmaeon traced the anatomy of the nervous system, in which Anaxagoras described the sun as a burning rock, in which Inopedes correctly calculated the angle at which the earth is inclined relative to the plane of its orbit, in which numbers of others including Archimedes, Hero (inventor of a prototype steam engine), and the physicians who used the electric shocks delivered by torpedo fish to stimulate the hearts of sick patients, showed that the classical world was on the brink of science. The advances in technology of the Roman phase of classical antiquity, most remarkably in engineering, carry the story forward in an applied direction. There is an interesting comparison to be made between the practicality and pragmatism of the Chinese and Romans and the theoretical understanding sought by the Greeks. If a methodology of experimentation had resulted from a marriage between the *praxis* and *gnosis* of that epoch, the true scientific revolution of the late Renaissance (the 16th and 17th centuries CE) could well have occurred a millennium and a half earlier.

The second point concerns the dark age introduced by the success of Christianity, this latter in a trajectory from, approximately speaking, the late fourth to the early sixteenth centuries of the Common Era, the darkest centuries being the fifth to the eleventh. Above I used the example of the loss of knowledge that meant nothing like the Basilica of Maxentius (308–12 CE) could be built in Italy until Brunelleschi's dome for Florence's Duomo (1419–36 CE), but across the range of literature, philosophy, science, technology, painting, sculpture, the art of living itself, the best that the Dark Ages could produce – it produced some – fails to compare. Petrarch and the other movers of the Renaissance, a term they themselves coined to mean the rebirth of civilisation, also coined the term 'Middle Ages' to denote the period between their own rediscovery of the ancient world and the ancient world itself. It was a conscious reawakening, and the degree to which it succeeded in opening minds and encouraging independence of thought was what made the 16th and 17th century scientific and philosophical revolutions, and they in turn the 18th century Enlightenment and the modern world, eventually possible. I say all this in the most schematic form here; in two books, *What is Good* (2002) and *Towards the Light* (2007) I say more.

Note this fact therefore: it was not until the seventeenth and eighteenth centuries of the Common Era, with the renewed rise of science and the Enlightenment it prompted, that the course set by the philosophers of antiquity was properly resumed. If we are indeed in an early phase of human history, historians ten thousand years from now might see this period of interruption in the first major chapter of humanity's progress as a blip, a temporary distraction as humanity tried to shed the cocoon of its earliest superstitions.

As so often, the Greeks themselves understood with a preternatural clarity the nature of the turning point they represented in this story. Aeschylus says much of what the preceding paragraphs have been saying, but in other words: the words of his play *Prometheus Bound*. Prometheus stole fire from the gods and gave it to mankind, 'a measureless resource for man, and mighty teacher of all arts'; and for making man powerful in this way, and no longer dependent on the gods' favour – for helping mankind towards its maturity and self-reliance, and thus promising to free it from subjection to religion – Prometheus was punished by Zeus, who bound him to a rock on a high mountain, and set an eagle to gnaw his liver every day, the liver regrowing at night in preparation for the next day's torture.

The idea of freeing the world from the tyranny of religion can be therefore be symbolised as the task of setting free Prometheus himself. Hence the title of this book. In choosing it I follow Shelley's version of the myth, expressed in the introduction to his *Prometheus Unbound,* having it that Prometheus's liberation represents the overthrow of 'mankind's oppressor', that is, Zeus. In this Shelley was right as regards the philosophical truth that the myth reaches towards, for there can be no reconciliation, only victory to one side or other, in this titanic struggle – which is not a struggle between gods and men, for there are no gods, but rather between man and the religions he invents out of ignorance, fear, and desire for power, with which to oppress others and his own mind.

2

Why I do not subscribe to religious beliefs

'It is not what the man of science believes that
distinguishes him, but how and why he believes
it. His beliefs are tentative, not dogmatic; they are
based on evidence, not on authority or intuition.'

BERTRAND RUSSELL

IN COMMON PARLANCE, 'to be a believer' means
having a religious faith. We all have many non-
religious beliefs, but what distinguishes them from
the beliefs that amount to religious faith is the kind
of grounds on which we hold them, and the nature
of what they are about. Rather than say, 'Why I do
not subscribe to a religious faith' I might better say,
'Why I subscribe to a naturalistic world view', which
is more pertinent; to hold a naturalistic world view
is to exclude any kind of supernaturalistic, mystical,
faith-involving element.

From this it will in turn be obvious that by 'religion' I mean the standard thing and its offshoots:
a set of beliefs in one or more (generally personal)

supernatural agencies, typically a deity or set of deities, together with the values and practices taken to be entailed by the existence of any such, such as worship of it or them, submission and obedience to the supposed commands or requirements emanating from it or them, and so familiarly on. There are loose uses of 'religion' as in 'football is his religion' which are at best metaphorical, but always strictly a misuse of the term, and they are accordingly excluded.

In its focal and standard sense, 'religion' not only denotes a metaphysical commitment to the existence of something non-natural in, or somehow outside but connected to, the universe, but further that this something's relation to the universe is in some way significant – centrally, by being some or all of the universe's creator, ruler, and moral instructor. The meaning of these remarks is of course only notional – as with a lot of theological and religious discourse it is hard to attach a literal sense to what is claimed, which votaries defend by appealing to the ineffability of religious 'truths' and the finitude of our minds in comparison – but they vaguely indicate what religious people claim to believe.

One has to say something along the foregoing lines when discussing religion because religious apologists are inveterately apt to defend against criticism or refutation by saying, 'That is not what I mean by religion' and 'I don't recognise that caricature of what I believe'. Part of the sleight of hand at work here becomes obvious when one notes the great difference between what ordinary votaries of a religion believe and what their theologians and high priests say. For example: the ordinary church-going Christian has a more or less vague conception of a somewhat human-like, only grander, being or beings – God the 'father', Jesus, Mary, the 'Holy Ghost', saints and angels, and so forth – and they believe or think they believe in some literally true (though literally meaningless or contradictory) propositions about them such as that God became man, was born of a virgin, was killed but after a couple of days came back to life, and then 'rose into heaven' – some aspect of a physical increase of altitude from the surface of the earth residually involved – whereas if you speak to a theologian you will find that, in the complexified and polysyllabic rarifications of his craft, at least not all these things are to be taken literally, but have metaphorical or mystical interpretations, though the grounds on which bits of the story are to be cherry-picked for literal truth and which are to be treated as metaphor are moot.

Likewise, the fact that mythologies antedating Christianity are full of stories of gods impregnating mortal maids who give birth to heroic figures, not a few of whom go down into the underworld and return – think of Zeus and his dalliances with at least 27 recorded mortal women, among them Alcmene, Antiope, Callisto, Danae, Electra, Europa, Io, Lamia, Leda, Niobe, Olympias and Semele, producing Hercules, Castor and Pollux, Helen of Troy, Alexander of Macedon, Lacedaemon, Minos, Rhadamanthus, Dardanus, and a number of other egregious figures of legend and history – makes it puzzling why anyone should think that the God-Mary-Jesus story is out of the ordinary, instead of what it is: merely an obvious borrowing and adaptation. Viewed in this light, and extended to religion in general, one sees that it is a function of historical accident that some people should today think they are consuming the body and blood of a god (the contradiction explained away by the doctrine of incarnation), some literally and some metaphorically, rather than slitting the throats of bulls and making libations to mountain-dwelling deities rather than heaven-dwelling ones.

But to revert to the main task in hand: I do not accept the metaphysics, nor therefore the attendant attitudes and practices, of religious belief, and what follows explains why.

The explanation I give is of why I reject claims to the effect that there are or might be supernatural aspects to the universe. It is not an explanation of why I reject as mere tales and myths the Olympian gods, the gods of Babylon, the Hindu pantheon, and so endlessly on, for as the foregoing remarks imply, it is just plainly obvious that all the historical religions are a hangover from the less knowledgeable and more superstitious infancy of mankind, or at least from that chapter of it in which what had been early science and technology – explanation of natural phenomena by appeal to the actions of purposive agents in nature, plus a 'technology' of prayer, sacrifice and taboo to influence these agencies – had begun to be abstracted into belief in mountain or sky (or anyway, far-off) deities as a result of the increase of knowledge which pushed those earlier proto-scientific efforts at explanation beyond the horizon. That religion as thus shaped survives is a well-recorded result of priest-hoods and temporal powers needing and supporting each other in order to control majority populations; the institutionalisation of religion, and the indoctrination of children into its tenets, are the joint reasons why it persists.

The fact that the major religions contradict and indeed blaspheme one another, a fact not lost on our forebears who went to war over it frequently, is however not taken by anyone to disprove all of them – it only disproves 'all of the others not mine'. So it goes.

But in any event, the particular religions – the incoherent mass of over twenty thousand Christian sects between them 'believing' an almost as large number of absurdities, the simple-minded and equally absurd beliefs of the dozens of sects of Islam, the fairy-tale legends and stories of Hinduism, and so on – would none of them recommend themselves to an ordinarily intelligent adult (not suffering grief or divorce or some other psychological trauma that the religions use as a portal to credulity) if he were first presented with them without any childhood predisposing by society and schooling. Asked to believe that they are true and important, and to base his life on them, such an adult would almost certainly feel one of two things: very amused, or very insulted.

And since all this is so, what follows is not about any particular 'revealed' or historical religion, but the basis of religious belief as such. It is, though, tiresome that one has to undertake the task at all, given that religion just is its manifestations in the 'revealed' historical religions, whose infantilisms, absurdities and obvious inheritance from a superstitious and ignorant remote past should surely be enough to make the conversation unnecessary.

The essential point for me is the rationality of belief. Suppose I reason as follows: 'Every time I have gone out of doors in the rain without an umbrella, I have got wet. But my belief that I will get wet next time I am so circumstanced is merely inductive; all past instances of getting wet in the rain without an umbrella do not jointly entail that the next time will be the same. So the next time it rains I will not take an umbrella because there is a chance that I will not get wet.' I take it that anyone who reasoned thus would merit being regarded as irrational. This implies that a principal mark of rationality is reliance on evidence, conformity with relevant experience, and respect for associated knowledge and theory (in this instance, about water and wetness).

Moreover, what I think would be rational to believe and do as regards umbrellas and rain is something I think in the light of knowing about the chicken who was fed every day until the day that his neck was wrung. That is, I understand the difference between beliefs and expectations which are warranted by the additional premises that can be adduced in one's acceptance and application of them, and those that are not. The rationality of a belief is a function of, among other things, the cumulative rationality of beliefs that support or challenge it in a matrix of such.

I choose examples of contingent belief that we typically say are inductively based, though as it happens (and this is a different argument which makes no difference here) I think all arguments are enthymematically deductive in the presence of over-arching generalisations serving as major premises, themselves rationally evaluable and supported by the success, rational and empirical, of the subordinate inferences they license, in a virtuous circle.[1] In the view of some who have thought about induction and rationality, the solution to the so-called 'problem of induction' is to see the justification of inductive infer-ences as residing in the rationality of acceptance of their conclusions.[2] The significance of such a view is not so much whether it solves the traditional problem of induction as that it explains the following crucial fact: why a typically rational individual would answer 'No' to the question, 'Do you believe that fairies exist' and 'Yes' to the question, 'Do you believe that water molecules exist', and not (for example) 'It is more

1   A close analogy is the 'covering law' model. See A. C. Grayling *Scepticism and the Possibility of Knowledge* London 2008 final chapter.

2   This is the tack taken by P. F. Strawson in *Introduction to Logical Theory* London 1952 Chapter 9 part II *passim*.

probable that water molecules exist than that fairies exist', or 'I attach a low probability to the existence of fairies and a high probability to the existence of water molecules'. This is an important point which needs explanation, as follows.

The Bayesian fashion in epistemology obliges its votaries to say that belief is not an all or nothing affair, a matter of 'yes' and 'no', but of degrees of belief calibrated as a subjective probability distribution over ranges of possibilities as to how the world might be in some relevant respect. A virtue of this approach is taken to be that it explains how people constantly adjust the weight they give to various of their beliefs as the supporting evidence waxes and wanes in strength, usually as more information comes to hand. People might not expressly think in terms of probabilities except when challenged to say just how much credence they give some claim, but their beliefs are nevertheless graduated by how probable they seem to their holder, and this is the fundamental epistemological fact of life. So says the Bayesian.

Now if this were indeed so, no self-respecting individual could say 'I do not believe in fairies/ unicorns/Olympian deities', and by this quite plainly mean, 'There are no such things as fairies/unicorns/ Olympian deities'. Instead he has to say, 'I attach a very low probability to there being such things as fairies/unicorns/Olympian deities'. Yet if we met someone who thought that it is very unlikely that there are such things instead of that there are no such things, we would not regard him as rational, but as an idiot. This is because whether it is rational or not to believe something is indeed an all or nothing affair, and not a matter of degree. It is of course the case that it is sometimes uncertain whether something is or is not so, and therefore rational to suspend judgment or to take a bet on whatever probability evaluation one can make; and doubtless this happens when the probability of that something's being the case is around .5. But it is not rational to take a bet on something's being the case that has a probability of .99-recurring of not being the case, and since acceptance of and action upon a belief is exactly comparable to taking a bet, the questions 'is it rational to bet on x' and 'is it rational to believe in x' alike admit of unequivocal yes-no answers.

The initial probability of there being 'a deity', by the way, is not .5 as some like to try to argue. Instead it is of the first interest to ask what initial probability one would attach to the existence of (say) tree nymphs, or unicorns, or anything else whose presence in fable, legend, myth and religion is the product of what ancient people have handed down as their stories about the world. Whatever that number is, if it is not 0 then it is vanishingly close to 0. The mistake made by many is to think that because a particular such tradition has been institutionalised, that fact somehow increases the probability that the entities referred to in its discourse is any greater than 0 or vanishingly close to it. But this is an aside suggested by the mistake of thinking that the key thing about belief is probability rather than rationality. It is a pernicious mistake; it allows religious apologists to wriggle into the tiny gap left by the point-millions-of-zeroes-one probability that the proposition 'god exists' (whatever that means) is true, and to base themselves on it – as Pascal did. Whether it is rational to disbelieve and act accordingly, rational to believe and act accordingly, or rational to suspend judgment and act in whatever prudential way seems best on the fractional likelihoods either way, is a clear-cut matter; and in connection with fairies, unicorns, deities *et hoc genus omne*, the clear-cut option is the first.

This is because of the sheer weight of evidence and reason that makes it so. The evidence comes from common experience, applied and practical endeavour (as in the historical emergence of farming techniques, construction of buildings, medical practice, and so on), and organised scientific investigation. In the first two cases the responsible norm, and in the case of science the professional requirement, is that what we think and do must be proportioned to the evidence (*ratio*-nally) available, including the long-term outcome of trial and error in the first two cases and the disciplined, public and repeatable experimentation and assessment of predicted outcomes in the third. There is in each kind of case a systematic requirement for identifying what counts as evidence, how it is tested, what constitutes support for or challenge to hypotheses, and how much confidence can be placed in conclusions arrived at. Different fields of enquiry impose different requirements, but the collective epistemological endeavour in each imposes stringent controls. The paradigm is science, which institutionalises publicity, repeatability, and peer-review of experiment and test, and is as a matter of strict principle defeasible in the face of evidence.

A great deal can be said about what all this further means, but two points are salient. One is that the views and practices that emerge from common sense, practicality and science form a general picture of a law-like natural realm in which we know what it is rational to believe and do, and what is not. We know that, for example, it is rational to expect that we can light and heat a house by installing the right kinds of appliances in it and connecting them to a power source such as an electricity grid, and at the same time we know that it is irrational to believe that we can light and heat it by prayer alone, or by sacrificing a white heifer and dancing round its entrails. This is precisely and exactly why it is rational to believe the deliverances of common sense, practicality and science, and irrational to believe religious claims: the former are based on evidence massively gathered and confirmed by experience, whereas the various etiolated fancies constituting the latter are untestable, inconsistent with each other, internally contradictory, and in conflict with the deliverances of common sense and science.

Some who would try to give room for two 'magisteria' repudiate the last remark made, arguing for a form of mutual consistency by construing religion and science as incommensurable discourses which address and operate in wholly disjoint spheres. That is heroic, but will not wash: the religions make existential claims about what is in or attached to the universe and putatively make a huge difference to it – claims that are unverifiable by and at odds with science and common sense. In fact religion and science are competitors for the truth about such things as the origins of the universe, the nature of humankind, and the ways that the laws of nature can be locally and temporarily suspended so that (for example) a prophet can kill large numbers of opponents (see for example Numbers 16.30 and the rest of the Bible passim). Effort to arrange a test that would adjudicate between these competing claims will always be won by science, but the votaries of the faiths will always have a convenient escape clause such as 'God will not be tested' and the like.

It is surely fruitless to press this aspect of the matter, once one has said: contrast the current state of geology and evolutionary biology with commitment to belief in a six-day creation that occurred six thousand years ago. This single example of the staring difference between disciplined rationality and what is nothing short of pathological irrationality ought to be enough, in its generalisation to all religious belief, to settle the matter – and among other things to outlaw the abuse of children by allowing them to be taught religious dogma and tradition as fact rather than as one of the often more tragic aspects of history.

But one ought always to conclude this aspect of the discussion by invoking Karl Popper's shade, whose remark that 'a theory which explains everything explains nothing' should be the rationalist mantra.

Religious claims are irrefutable because untestable; nothing will be accepted as counter-evidence by the faithful, neither the existence of natural and moral evil, nor the deliverances of science and reason; there is always an excuse or an explanation, or the last scoundrelly resort to claims about the ineffability or mystery of divinity, so that even the grossest conflicts with the facts or logic can be explained away or discounted by those who want so very much to believe that they are willing to dispense with a significant part of their mental capacity.

The nature of religious belief, the reasons for it, and the reasons for its persistence, are all explicable without any need to suppose the truth of any part of it. This conforms to Ockham's Razor. In brief: two general sources of belief can be mooted. One, already mentioned, is that among earliest man proto-science and proto-technology consisted in explaining natural occurrences by analogy with man's own agency and purposes, and by efforts to modify the intentions and emotions of that agency by propitiation or observance of taboo, and the like. As knowledge increased, so the agencies were conceived in ever more abstract terms, eventually having to be relocated altogether from nature into a supernatural realm. This probably happened because the vested interests of a priesthood wished to retain the status and influence of being mediators with those agencies, no doubt in collusion with temporal powers where these existed.

Another reason is that hallucinogenic fungi, accidentally-at-first fermented food or liquids, exhaustion, fever, epilepsy or insanity, probably acted as vectors interpreted by ignorance as access to another reality, readily enough interpreted as the reality of the agencies controlling the world. Once either or a combination of these sources of religion had begun to be institutionalised, there was no looking back; and indeed never has been since, even with the young religions of Christianity and Islam which are syncretistic inheritors of their predecessors.

There is a difference as regards Christianity, though; the public religions of Greece and Rome that preceded it were state observances aimed at social and political cohesion, and did not include personal spiritual intercourse with a deity in private prayer and meditation. This latter was a psychological dimension added perhaps from traditions of mystical intoxication, trance and meditation from elsewhere in the historical wellsprings of faith, because the early history of Christianity was a largely secret one, lacking the large-scale outward celebrations of the Roman cults.

Once Christianity had attracted women and slaves in the Roman world, and from there the Roman world itself, and once one of its many different sects had captured the support of the Roman state machinery (and soon enough the machinery itself) and was able to impose itself as orthodoxy, the history of Christianity and the world was set on its now familiar course. For so many centuries it permeated the culture and institutions of society, dominated education, and resisted (to the point of murder and full-scale war) efforts to supplant its intellectual and moral authority, that even today in more rather than less secular western Europe it continues to be a large presence on the public scene.

The main key to the survival of all religions is their proselytisation of the young. For good evolutionary reasons children are highly credulous, believing in everything from the tooth fairy and Father Christmas to whatever gods the adults in their circle tell them to believe in. But whereas the tooth fairy and Father Christmas soon enough leave the scene along with fairies and trolls, god or the gods remain, reinforced by parental, educational and social institutionalistation. That this is a form of child abuse is unquestionable, not least because most of those who abandon religious faith later have a psychological and sometimes a social struggle to do so, often painful; and beforehand they may suffer agonies of apprehension and doubt because of their sexual feelings and consciousness of 'sin' in respect of all sorts of things that are natural and acceptable except in the eyes of the faith. The distorted lives of the victims of religion are plain to see from the Bible Belt of the United States to the veiled and shrouded women of Saudi Arabia and Afghanistan; genital mutilation, 'honour killings', forced marriages, and dozens of other abuses are perpetuated in the name of religion and tradition and contrary to rationality and humanity; the toll is great, and constitutes an indictment of religion as by far one of the least happy inventions of human ingenuity.

In more secular parts of the world where religions are on the back foot, their votaries assume a smiling face and an innocent posture. The Christian churches in the Western world no longer murder their opponents at the stake or in Crusading massacres, but offer the Kiss of Friendship to new members during church services. They concentrate on charity, peace and goodwill, a far cry from their past blood-soaked efforts to force everyone into obedience and submission. But this only applies when they are weak; where they are strong they are not so kid-gloved. The Taliban in Afghanistan offer an example of what all religions everywhere tend towards when given the opportunity: control, and imposition of orthodoxy and orthopraxy. This is not a merely rhetorical claim: the Christianity of the Inquisition, the Calvinists, the Puritans, is no different in practical effect from the Wahhabis of Saudi Arabia or the Taliban of Afghanistan.

Some of the votaries of Islam, keen on the return of the Caliphate, make no secret of their disdain for 'kaffirs' and their preparedness to kill and die for their faith. The mobs of chanting, self-flagellating Muslims stirred into a rabble by cartoons that poke fun at their Prophet, the riots of Hindus and Muslims beating each other to death on the streets of India, and suicide bombers in any part of the world, are evidence of the infantilism and irrationality to which religion can drive people. No other phenomenon comes close, except for the massed ranks of Nazis or the dutiful crowds at Soviet rallies. The comparisons are not accidental; what religions have in common with these is that they are all monolithic ideologies that claim the One Great Truth, to which everyone must subscribe on pain of punishment.

The contrast is with pluralism, individual liberty, consensual institutions, regimes of law and rights – in short, Enlightenment dispensations, in which it is not a crime but an obligation to think for oneself, be informed, allow disagreement, encourage debate, and tolerate differences. That is not religion's historical way, or its present way when it has the option. Just as science and religion are in direct competition for factual truth, so Enlightenment and religion are in direct competition when it comes to the contrasting kinds of society they envisage and work towards.

We can give thanks to those who struggled against the hegemony of religion that the possibility exists in many parts of the world for people to live free of it. Compare the lives of the majority of our ancestors in medieval times: illiterate, bound to the local soil, their only source of instruction, entertainment and art their visit to their parish church on Sundays and holidays. There the murals depicting the punishment of sinners in hellfire (see the grotesquely coercive imagery of these murals in the Alte Pinakothek in Munich, which has the paradigm collection of such) and the threats and adjurations of the priests, together with the filtered version of the dogma then taught, constituted the whole learning and understanding of the peasantry. That was a prison for the mind so complete, so dominating and coercive, that nothing existed outside it. And in any case to question it, if that was even possible without resources to think differently, was to invite death. At most two centuries have passed in two thousand years during which this mind-shackle of super-stition has not been completely the norm; and only one century in which it has been possible, without inviting at very least social opprobrium, to proclaim publicly one's opposition to it. But this latter applies only in the West; most people in most Islamic parts of the world suffer from a form of mental and social imprisonment today indistinguishable from that of Christianity's subjects in most of its history.

And one could go on, in explaining why one is 'not a believer', to examine the grounds on which religious apologists base their claims – the texts and traditions, the alleged 'mystical experiences' and revelations – and the psychological sources in childhood brainwashing, self-deception, reluctance to think, desire for author-ity, social pressure, and the vulnerabilities and fears on which the religious rely for recruitment.

Take just one thought, about the text on which Christians mainly base their faith: the Bible. In this confused, contradictory and tendentious document, the component 'books' are very obviously of their time, limited and frequently incorrect in the know-ledge they display, as well as largely incredible (the miracle stories, for a prime example), and equally frequently morally unappealing, not to say often despicable. A straightforward reading of any of the texts taken as especially important to the religions associated with them, such as the Koran and the Vedas, invites the same reaction. David Hume wryly remarked that those who thought the age of miracles had come to an end in biblical times were wrong, for it is – he said – a miracle that anyone continues to believe the bible stories. His point has all the greater force given that a frank reading of the world's supposed holy books is a powerful disincentive to any of the religions associated with them.

This scratches the surface of why I not only reject the claims of religion, but think religion ought to be opposed and contested because it consists of falsehood and distortion, and is harmful to humanity. In response to those who point at the comfort some versions of it now give the old, the lonely and the fearful, I respond by saying that the rich, deep and responsible ethics of humanism are a far better resource for human fellowship, for it is based on kindness and truth, and does not trade on falsehoods about the world tiptoeing on the hidden cleft hooves of 'faith'.

If there is one practical move I would advocate towards diminishing the place of religion in human affairs, it is shriving education of it: that is the key to a better future.

3

Why Bertrand Russell was not religious

R USSELL WROTE MUCH and repeatedly about religion, and an examination of what he had to say
yields surprising results for anyone whose knowledge
of his views stops at knowing only that he did not
believe in the existence of a god or gods, and that he
was a trenchant opponent of organised religion and
a castigator of what he saw as its harmful effects on
human individuals and society. All this is true; but
what is even more interesting is that he was deeply
concerned to find an alternative to religion as a source
of value and a motivator to action aimed at the good.
He wrote. 'I am constantly asked: What can you, with
your cold rationalism, offer to the seeker after salva-
tion that is comparable to the cosy homelike comfort
of a fenced dogmatic creed?' (*The Impact of Science on
Society* p. 87); and the person who most often asked
him this question was: Russell himself.

When in that same passage he continued, 'To this
the answer is many-sided' (ibid.) he was adverting to
the fact that he had tried, and was then in the midst

of trying, to find what one might best call a humanistic alternative. This was not an expression he himself used, but it is the closest term in the current lexicon of debate that captures his intentions. The trajectory of his endeavour started with the high-minded sentiments and purple prose of his essay 'A Free Man's Worship' (written in 1902–3) and ended long before he described in his intellectual autobiography *My Philosophical Development* (1959) the conclusion he had reached, that although the desire for an overarching source of value is a powerful and motivating human yearning, it is not a response to anything external to itself.

Before examining the two aspects of Russell on religion – his sharply critical attacks on religion and religious belief themselves, and his search for a humanistic alternative – one preliminary must be disposed of. This is Russell's self-description as an 'agnostic' rather than an atheist. His own definition of the terms shows what he meant. In the essay 'What is an Agnostic?' he defines the term thus: 'An agnostic is a man who thinks it is impossible to know the truth in matters such as God and future life with which the Christian religion and other religions are concerned, or, if not for ever impossible, at any rate impossible at present'. He then proceeds to define 'atheist' thus: 'Are agnostics atheists? No. An atheist, like a Christian, holds that we can know whether or not there is a God. The Christian holds that we can know there is a God, the atheist that we can know there is not. The agnostic suspends judgment, saying that there are not sufficient grounds either for affirmation or for denial. At the same time, an agnostic may hold that the existence of God, though not impossible, is very improbable; he may even hold that it is so improbable that it is not worth considering in practice. In that case, he is not far removed from atheism. His attitude may be that which a careful philosopher would have towards the gods of ancient Greece. If I were asked to prove that Zeus and Poseidon and Hera and the rest of the Olympians do not exist, I should be at a loss to find conclusive arguments. An agnostic may think the Christian God as improbable as the Olympians; in that case he is, for practical purposes, at one with the atheists' (ibid.).

This latter, then, was what Russell meant by calling himself an agnostic: he was 'at one with the atheists' but felt bound by logic to admit that he would be at a loss to find arguments to disprove the existence of the Olympian deities. With this reservation his arguments in criticism of religion and religious beliefs could proceed as if coming from the most trenchant of atheists.

Russell's position in this respect merits challenge. As a logician who in the decades after the publication of *Principia Mathematica* devoted so much effort to showing – in effect, and to use his own earlier terminology – how science, as knowledge by description, can be derived ultimately from knowledge by acquaintance, he should have distinguished between proof in a formal deductive system (demonstrative proof) and proof in the empirical setting (scientific proof). The former consists in deriving a conclusion from premises by rules, and are literally explications in the sense that all the information constituting the conclusion already exists in the premises, so a derivation is in fact a rearrangement. There is no logical novelty in the conclusion, though often enough there is psychological novelty, in the sense that the conclusion can seem unobvious or even surprising if the information constituting it was highly dispersed among the premises.

Demonstrative proof is watertight and conclusive. It is a mechanical matter; computers do it best. Change the rules or axioms of a formal system, and you change the results. Such proof is only to be found in mathematics and logic.

Proof in all other spheres of reasoning, and paradigmatically in science, consists in adducing evidence of the kind and in the quantity that makes it irrational, absurd, irresponsible or even a mark of insanity to reject the conclusion thus being supported. The definitive illustration of what this means, not least for the use that theists would like to make of the myth that 'you cannot prove a negative', is Carl Sagan's dragon-in-the-garage story.[3] On this basis someone who on the basis of evidence and reasoning concludes that it is irrational, absurd, irresponsible or even lunatic to believe that there is such a thing as deity, might further ask whether it is nevertheless none of these things to believe that there might be such a thing as deity. Consider an analogy. Suppose someone thinks: 'My belief that rain will wet me if I do not use an umbrella is (only?) inductively justified; therefore I am entitled to believe that it is possible that rain might not wet me next time I do not use an umbrella when it rains.' Is the belief that 'rain might not wet me next time' less irrational or absurd than the belief that rain does not wet at all? Obviously not. For this reason Russell's use of 'agnostic' as functionally equivalent to 'atheist' but with the reservation of a quibble about proof is seen to turn on an assimilation of proof concerning

---

3   Reference: http://www.users.qwest.net/~jcosta3/article_dragon.htm.

matters of fact to proof of the demonstrative kind – and it is a quibble that does not, *pace* our man with the umbrella, hold water.

Pointing this out matters because misapprehensions about the nature of proof continue to support the apparent plausibility of agnosticism. But agnosticism, as the position that entertains the possibility that there might be or could be one or more supernatural agencies of some sort, is an irrational position, for precisely the same reason as holding that there might be or could be fairies or goblins or the Olympian deities or the Norse gods. For this reason Russell on his own grounds ought to have recognised that he was entitled to declare himself an atheist, just as he was entitled by argument to announce that he was not a Christian. And indeed, at times he did indeed describe himself as an atheist, as when, in a wry remark in the passage in his autobiography where he talks about nearly having died from pneumonia in China in 1921, he writes, 'I was told that the Chinese said they would bury me in the Western Lake and build a shrine to my memory. I regret that this did not happen, as I might have become a god, which would have been very chic for an atheist.'

We can now turn to the two substantive matters involved in Russell's thought about religion – namely, his objections to it, and his quest for an alternative – beginning with the first.

Russell's attack on religious belief took a variety of forms and was expressed in a variety of ways, often in the form of ridiculing the contradictions, absurdities and anthropocentric parochialisms of religions and their sacred texts, practices and ethics, and sometimes in the form of direct argumentation against the claims either of natural theology or revelation. He also argued from more general historical and sociological considerations about the effects of religion – and more generally 'faith' understood as including not just religion but Soviet Communism and the like – on society and human lives. He saw that religions and political tyrannies share in common a monolithic structure which demands subservience and loyalty on pain of punishment, proscribes independence of thought and action, hands down the dogma to be believed and lived by, and issues a one-size-fits-all morality or way of life to which conformity must be absolute. Russell objected both intellectually and morally, and both on principle and in defence of human nature and possibility, to the harm done by this. The tenor of his attacks on religion is explainable accordingly.

The rhetorical technique of refutation by exposing absurdity is by no means an illegitimate one, consisting as it does in focusing attention on claims and their consequences as a way of inspecting their merits. To take just a couple of many examples; in *A History of Western Philosophy* Russell writes: 'According to St. Thomas the soul is not transmitted with the semen, but is created afresh with each man. There is, it is true, a difficulty: when a man is born out of wedlock, this seems to make God an accomplice in adultery. This objection, however, is only specious. There is a grave objection which troubled St. Augustine, and that is as to the transmission of original sin. It is the soul that sins, and if the soul is not transmitted, but created afresh, how can it inherit the sin of Adam? This is not discussed by St. Thomas.' (ibid. p. 458) Again: 'I am sometimes shocked by the blasphemies of those who think themselves pious – for instance, the nuns who never take a bath without wearing a bathrobe all the time. When asked why, since no man can see them, they reply: "Oh, but you forget the good God." Apparently they conceive of the Deity as a Peeping Tom, whose omnipotence enables Him to see through bathroom walls, but who is foiled by bathrobes. This view strikes me as curious.' (*Unpopular Essays* pp. 75–6)

The principal objection Russell had to religion is its deleterious effect on individuals and society. The harm to individuals was both intellectual and moral, as he respectively points out thus: 'What I wish to maintain is that all faiths do harm. We may define "faith" as a firm belief in something for which there is no evidence. When there is evidence, no one speaks of "faith". We do not speak of faith that two and two are four or that the earth is round. We only speak of faith when we wish to substitute emotion for evidence.' (*Human Society in Ethics and Politics* p. 215) 'There is something feeble and a little contemptible about a man who cannot face the perils of life without the help of comfortable myths. Almost inevitably some part of him is aware that they are myths and that he believes them only because they are comforting. But he dare not face this thought! Moreover, since he is aware, however dimly, that his opinions are not rational, he becomes furious when they are disputed.' (ibid. pp. 219–20)

Pointing out the absurdity of belief and the harm done by its institutionalisation is a more potent way of combating it than by rebutting arguments for the existence of God, which is a major topic of debate in philosophy of religion. But Russell addressed these arguments too, a number of times, although he was satisfied that Kant had demolished them all long before in the *Critique of Pure Reason*. He dismissed the First Cause argument on the ground that if the claim that everything must have a cause can only be prevented from collapsing into infinite regress by accepting that there is a self-caused first cause, then there is no reason to invoke the notion of a God since the world could just as well be its own first cause. But in fact, said Russell, the First Cause argument is just a version of one that says that the world rests on an elephant and the elephant on a tortoise, and that if you ask what the tortoise rests on, well, let's just change the subject: 'The argument is really no better than that'. (*Why I Am Not a Christian* pp. 6–7)

Russell was as summary with the so-called 'Argument from Design', saying that he found it impossible to believe that omnipotence and omniscience, with all the hundreds of millions of years available to it, should have produced so many imperfections and design flaws as are manifest in the world, or so much cruelty, as any visit to a children's ward in a hospital would show – making Nero 'a saint' in comparison to a deity who could create such a world (ibid. pp. 61–2). In Russell's view the Argument from Design was the religious apologist's principal argument, and he repeatedly assaulted and ridiculed it, describing it as 'a very poor argument indeed' which – as he also repeatedly remarked – was shown by physics to be false because our planet is destined to be destroyed in the natural course of the sun's enlargement and eventual extinction, making the idea of a providential creation and design of life on it a nonsense (ibid.).

Nor could Russell accept the view that the idea of a deity was needed to bring justice into the world, on the ground that since injustice seems to be so richly rewarded in this life, a next life is required to provide a remedy by giving the just their reward. But if one were thinking scientifically about the evidence, the presence of injustice in this world would be good grounds for inferring that there is as much injustice anywhere else, just as the presence of rotten oranges at the top of a crate makes it probable that there are more rotten oranges deeper down in the crate (ibid. p. 64).

The somewhat more usual argument to the necessity of God for morality is that without the former you cannot have the latter. The version of this argument that Russell criticised in his essay 'Is There A God?' is one popularised by William James. Russell wrote, 'The first and greatest objection to this argument is that, at its best, it cannot prove that there is a God but only that politicians and educators ought to try to make people think there is one'. A second objection is that 'Many of the best men known to history have been unbelievers. John Stuart Mill may serve as an instance. And many of the worst men known to history have been believers. Of this there are innumerable instances. Perhaps Henry VIII may serve as typical.'

For Russell the chief motivation to religious belief is not argument of the kind just discussed and dismissed, but the result of being taught in infancy the religion of whatever community one happens to be born into (ibid.) and thereafter being afraid to abandon that belief because of insecurity, anxieties about death, and the need for comfort (ibid. p. 70). These are non-rational and often irrational considerations, and therefore are not amenable to argument directed at proof or disproof. The point carries through even to those who putatively offer philosophical support for commitments of faith and its tenets, as Russell shows in criticising Aquinas, taken to be the greatest of religion's philosophers: 'There is little of the true philosophic spirit in Aquinas. He does not, like the Platonic Socrates, set out to follow wherever the argument may lead. He is not engaged in an inquiry, the result of which it is impossible to know in advance. Before he begins to philosophise, he already knows the truth; it is declared in the Catholic faith. If he can find apparently rational arguments for some parts of the faith, so much the better; if he cannot, he need only fall back on revelation. The finding of arguments for a conclusion given in advance is not philosophy, but special pleading.' (*HWP* p. 463)

For Russell it was close to sufficient to illustrate the action of religion in human affairs to reveal both its implausibility and unacceptability. The most systematic effort he made in this direction is his book *Religion and Science* ([*RS*] 1935). There he took the view that religion and science are direct competitors for the truth about the world, its origin, its nature, whether or not it exhibits purpose, and what can be inferred from it for ethics. One of the chief lessons to emerge, in Russell's view, is the necessity of accepting the deliverances of science and disciplining one's reasoning to its methods. Both here and in the essay 'An Outline of Intellectual Rubbish' (1943) Russell contrasted the growth of science with the efforts made by religion to impede that growth. 'Throughout the last 400 years, during which the growth of science had gradually shown men how to acquire knowledge of the ways of nature and mastery over natural forces, the clergy have fought a losing battle against science, in astronomy and geology, in anatomy and physiology, in biology and psychology and sociology. Ousted from one position, they have taken up another. After being worsted in astronomy, they did their best to prevent the rise of geology; they fought against Darwin in biology, and at the present time they fight against scientific theories of psychology and education. At each stage, they try to make the public forget their earlier obscurantism, in order that their present obscurantism may not be recognised for what it is.' (*RS* pp. 244 ff., *WINC* p. 208)

Such are the kinds of considerations that made Russell an opponent of religions and religious belief. What was equally important to him and even more interesting in itself was his attempt to articulate an alternative vision of the world and value that would do everything for mankind what some in mankind thought or hoped religion would do for it, but without religion's metaphysical irrationality and its moral and social distortions. This is what Russell early called 'a free man's worship', though he came to abandon the high-sounding ambitions for such a thing as his reflections on the matter matured.

To understand what Russell was after in this connection, it is important to notice that, in the absence of a ready term to denote what he meant, he gave a second but secular meaning to the term 'religion' to mean a sentiment or feeling which carries individuals out of themselves towards some overarching sense of value or purpose that transcends belittling self-concern. In his essay 'The Essence of Religion' (1912) he describes religion in this philosophical sense as a feeling which captures 'that quality of infinity' which gives rise to 'the selfless, untrammeled life in the whole which frees man from the prison house of eager wishes and thoughts'. Throughout his thinking on these matters Russell felt acutely the fact of the universe's indifference and crushingly superior power over the individual, as the blind play of natural forces working according to natural laws unfolded like a juggernaut without consciousness of the pain or pleasure felt by sentient beings, and man's possibility of a small but noble endeavour to sustain a commitment to value in the face of this fact.

In 'A Free Man's Worship' Russell had risen to dithyrambic heights in asserting this view: 'Brief and powerless is Man's life; on him and all his race the slow, sure doom falls pitiless and dark. Blind to good and evil, reckless of destruction, omnipotent matter rolls on its relentless way; for Man, condemned to-day to lose his dearest, to-morrow himself to pass through the gate of darkness, it remains only to cherish, ere yet the blow falls, the lofty thoughts that ennoble his little day; disdaining the coward terrors of the slave of Fate, to worship at the shrine that his own hands have built; undismayed by the empire of chance, to preserve a mind free from the wanton tyranny that rules his outward life; proudly defiant of the irresistible forces that tolerate, for a moment, his knowledge and his condemnation, to sustain alone, a weary but unyielding Atlas, the world that his own ideals have fashioned despite the trampling march of unconscious power.' Over thirty years later he was saying much the same thing far more soberly, in *Religion and Science*: 'The man who feels deeply the problem of human destiny, the desire to diminish the sufferings of mankind, and the hope that the future will realise the best possibilities of our species, is nowadays said to have a religious outlook…in so far as religion consists in a way of feeling, rather than in a set of beliefs, science cannot touch it.' The closest analogy Russell could find to express his view in the tradition of philosophy was, he said, Spinoza's idea of 'the intellectual love of God', but where there is no such thing as God and where nature is not substituted for God, but where a sense of the greater value of all things taken together – greater therefore than petty individual self-concern – serves as the target of the self-liberating emotional response Russell yearned for, and yearned to describe.

Indeed the best account given of this owes itself to Kenneth Blackwell in his *The Spinozistic Ethics of Bertrand Russell* (1985) where he writes, 'There is a similarity between Russell's concept derived from Spinoza of impersonal self-enlargement and the Buddhist concept of egolessness'. In *The Conquest of Happiness* (1930) Russell had made the idea of self-transcendence – now cast in more prosaic terms as having outward-looking interests and commitments – the key to personal happiness; the insight is a good one, of course, and an obvious one, a fact which has drawn the criticism of banality from those who did not realise that beneath it lay the deepest of Russell's ethical impulses.

The idea of the outward-looking, self-transcending stance expressed itself in two connected ways for Russell. One related to science, the other to personal relationships and the individual's attitude to others in general. In regard to science, the objectivity and scope of science is obviously such as to make individual self-concern a very minor if not indeed nugatory thing. In the essay 'The Place of Science in a Liberal Education' Russell wrote, 'The kernel of the scientific outlook is the refusal to regard our own desires and interest as affording the key to the understanding of the world', and this immediately entails that the disciplines of reason and evidence are the sole legitimate determinants of thinking in general. But in view of the potential that science has, via technology, to aggrandise and serve the lust for power which is all too constant a feature of human nature, there has to be a counterbalance, and this Russell identified in another human capacity, this time for love. In *The Impact of Science on Society* (1951), written at a time when the technological threats to human survival were mounting exponentially in the form of weapons of mass destruction, he wrote: 'The root of the matter is a very simple and old-fashioned thing, a thing so simple that I am almost ashamed to mention it, for fear of the derisive smile with which wise cynics will greet my words. The thing I mean – please forgive me for mentioning it – is love, Christian love, or compassion.' And he went on to add that if his reader felt such compassion 'you have all that anybody should need in the way of religion' (ibid.).

This last statement, written late in Russell's life and in the face of yet another threat – this time an even greater one – than all those that had drawn him to social and political action at various stages of his life, best captures what he desired by way of a practical alternative to religion. It looks far from the objective something-or-other which, because it is independent of individual human desires and weakness, can summon and even command the best from us and be the indisputable ground for action; rather, it is immanent and as fragile as its source; but it is all there is, and all that is anyway necessary.

After losing his faith as a teenager – an event recorded in an early diary and related in his autobiography – Russell never changed his views about religion, or about the need for an alternative to religion that would be ethically compelling. The absence of a suitable alternative vocabulary for articulating his thoughts in the latter respect made him talk of 'life in the spirit' and 'personal religion', but always in wholly secular terms, and it was in this sense that he once wrote: 'I consider some form of personal religion highly desirable and feel that many people are unsatisfactory through lack of it' ('Replies to Critics' in P. A. Schilpp *The Philosophy of Bertrand Russell* 1944).

He also there said that what he regarded as his own best statement of his views on religion in both the religious and secular senses of the term as he meant them, is the chapter entitled 'Religion and the Churches' in his First World War book *Principles of Social Reconstruction* (1916). In that chapter, after recounting the struggle of both science and individuals to free themselves from the hegemony of the church, Russell says, 'If a religious view of life and the world is ever to reconquer the thoughts and feelings of free-minded men and women, much that we are accustomed to associate with religion will have to be discarded. The first and greatest change that is required is to establish a morality of initiative, not a morality of submission, a morality of hope rather than of fear, of things to be done rather than of things to be left undone. It is not the whole duty of man to slip through the world so as to escape the wrath of God. The world is our world, and it rests with us to make a heaven or a hell.' And the vision that will underwrite the making of a human heaven on human earth is, says Russell, 'not one of occasional solemnity and superstitious prohibitions, it will not be sad or ascetic, it will concern itself little with rules of conduct. It will be inspired by a vision of what human life may be, and will be happy with the joy of creation, living in a large free world of initiative and hope. It will love mankind, not for what they are to the outward eye, but for what imagination shows that they have it in them to be.' (ibid.)

4

Scientists confront Intelligent Design and Creationism

S INCE THE HUMILIATING defeat of the creationist lobby in the Scopes Monkey Trial of 1925 in
Tennessee, religious groups have grown increasingly
sophisticated (in both senses of this term, to denote
more nuanced and organised, and more sophistical)
in their efforts to promote the idea that the universe
and life in this remote corner of it were made by an
intelligent agency, somewhat as a carpenter makes a
table; except that the putative mega-agency did not
have materials (the analogue of wood and nails) to
hand beforehand, but made them too, *ex nihilo*.

Thus literalist Six Day Creationism mutated
(evolved? or would it be too tendentious to employ
this term?) into new disguises, as 'Creation Science'
and – yet more sophisticatedly – Intelligent Design
theory. Creation Science purports to show that
the geological and fossil record is all explicable in
terms of a single act of creation by a suitable agency,

and a world-wide flood. On this view vegetarian Tyrannosaurus Rex shared Eden with Adam and Eve, and so great was the weight of waters in the Flood that what looks like aeons of geological strata were laid down in the short span of time between the rain and the dove's return with a (presumably wet?) twig of leaves in its beak.

Intelligent Design (ID) theory is more insidiously disguised, because it does not invoke either of the two creation myths in Genesis directly, but tries to argue on putative scientific grounds that there is irreducible complexity in nature that can only be explained as the outcome of intelligent design. Its proponents thereby construct a Trojan Horse for creationism by arguing that their theory, as a scientific theory, should have equal time in schools with Darwinian biology.

The naïve absurdities of creationism in any disguise, and the sophistries and dishonesties of ID, have received repeated setbacks in American courtrooms in recent years, as school boards in more backward States have tried to insinuate the religious agenda into the teaching of school science, only to be contested and consistently defeated by First Amendment defenders. The money, organisation, propaganda effort and persistence of the religious lobby is remarkable; entire 'institutes' to promote its agenda exist, a notable example being the richly funded 'Discovery Institute' in Seattle, which laughably describes itself in its promotional literature as 'a nonpartisan public policy think tank conducting research on technology, science and culture, economics and foreign affairs'. Ten seconds reading its home page gives the lie to any implication of neutrality and dispassion.

Back in the 1980s, before the renewed religion debate heated up to its present extent, distinguished anthropologist Laurie S. Godfrey edited a collection of essays entitled *Science Confronts Creationism* (1984), Twenty-three years later she returned, in company with Andrew J. Petto, to take up the cudgels again. The title of the later collection, *Scientists Confront Intelligent Design and Creationism* (2007) registers the evolution in religious efforts just described; whereas the earlier collection addressed creationism, the later one addressed both creationism and ID. The cancer, in short, had continued to spread. It scarcely needs saying that the essays Godfrey and Petto included are conclusive in their aims; what makes one shake one's head is the time, energy and effort these genuine scientists were obliged to direct towards combating the irresponsible absurdities of creationism and ID, distracting them from their real work because they have to defend their disciplines, and indeed American education, from the corrosive effects of disguised and confabulated versions of superstition.

It has to be confessed, though, that the essays make for entertaining reading. A prime example is the comprehensive and swingeing demolition by Victor J. Stenger of ID theory's darling, William Dembski, whose quite remarkably dishonest (or ignorant) manipulations of statistics and information theory to 'prove' that biological systems are too complex to have evolved naturally, have been ID's mainstay. This indeed is the key to the ID challenge, and essay after essay in the Godfrey and Petto volume powerfully shows how this is nothing but an argument from ignorance, usually the ID proponent's own.

The really surprising thing, though, is this. What is the value of saying, with respect to anything we do not, or do not yet, understand, that it was made by an invisible one-eyed toad – or pick any arbitrary supposed agent and call it what you like: Fred, or God, or Mother Goose? The child's question presses: viz. if the universe and life in this corner of it had to be designed by (say) Mother Goose, who is she that she could do such a thing? Is she complex, and therefore did she need a designer in her turn? If so, that designer must have been pretty complex too, of not indeed more so, and would need a fancier designer in its own turn…and so on *ad infinitum.* Explanatory regresses with no first term explain nothing. Or did Mother Goose design herself, and if so, how might that work? Just a snap of her antecedently non-existent fingers? (Might she have evolved from a gosling? and it from a goose egg? If so, whence the goose egg? Regress again.)

In short, the explanatory value of an arbitrary, plucked-out-of-thin-air idea of a designer or a deity or a Mother Goose to 'explain' the universe and the complexity of life in it is null. What possible sense do the votaries of such an arbitrary view think they are making? Well, of course, their entire effort is devoted to finding premises for an antecedently accepted conclusion; they know in advance the answer, and are trying to fabricate the right questions to get to it; they know what they regard as proved, and are searching for the proof, for suitable evidence to back it, or for ways of twisting evidence that otherwise leads to very different conclusions. They subscribe for non-rational reasons to one of many creation myths from the infancy of mankind, and are seeking for justifications in support of it. This is as far from science, rationality, and intellectual honesty, as you can get: and it is absolutely characteristic of the creationist/ID project.

The ID project addresses itself mainly to biology in opposition to evolutionary theory. Creation science addresses itself mainly to the physics of cosmogony and cosmology, on the origins and nature of the universe. They overlap when they invoke the fact that life could not exist on this planet unless the constants of nature were fine-tuned exactly as they are. To a mind naïvely seeking straws for a house of straw – viz. creationism/ID – the fact that the universe is fine-tuned for life is like Dr Pangloss's account of the nose: that it exists to support our spectacles. Dr Pangloss inferred the necessity of the nose from the existence of spectacles; he did not bother to consider other ways of remedying defects of vision, or note the many other facial arrangements which do not support spectacles as ours do, but nevertheless exist; and so on. Just so do the invokers of the anthropic principle fail to think there might be other forms of life possible in universes tuned to different constants, or many other universes anyway, or different phases in this one determined by different values of changing constants; and the like.

Again: what a waste of effort is here provoked by the necessity to quash absurdity. Take just one example in illustration. Creationists contest isotopic dating techniques which show that the earth is billions of years old by suggesting that 'since the Creation one or more episodes occurred when nuclear decay rates were billions of times greater than today's rates. Possibly there were three episodes: one in the early part of the Creation week, another between the Fall and the Flood, and the third during the year of the Genesis flood' (this from a publication by a creationist group calling itself RATE – 'Radioisotopes and the Age of the Earth'). Brent Dalrymple calmly points out that for this suggestion to be true some important things would have to be different: it would require changes in fundamental physical numbers including Planck's constant and the speed of light, which in turn changes the nature of light and many other physical and chemical properties. And if this were so the universe would no longer work as it does – or a very different one would result. Such is the quality of thought, which in understatement Dalrymple describes as 'incredibly naïve'.

Alas, while the folk of faith continue trying to urge their revisionary views, and no doubt succeed with the gullible and those anxious to bolster their convictions, the necessity will remain to contest them. The ancient tales are quick and easy to sell, the depth and complexity of real science takes effort to understand; all snake-oil purveyors have this asymmetry on their side. Thus it is that the contributors to Godfrey's and Petto's collection have to devote time to arguing that there are no fairies at the bottom of the garden. It is no wonder that the attitude of non-religious people is hardening against the persistently tiresome endeavours of the fairy-worshippers, making the debate a bad-tempered one. It is to the credit of most scientists forced to combat the purveyors of fairy tales that they generally remain cool, measured and conclusive throughout. When they do not, who can blame them?

5

The war of the books

THOUSANDS OF BOOKS on different aspects of religion are published every year. They range from works of theology to works of spiritual advice and exhortation, books on prayer, bible stories for children, uplifting memoirs of a religious bent, and more. (Put 'religion' into the Amazon search box and over 960,000 results are flagged. In the unlikely event that as many as 10 per cent of these are critical of religion, that leaves an awful – in all senses – lot of religion-purveying texts in circulation.)

In the last few years four books by tough-minded atheists have mounted the best-seller lists and caused an uproar: Sam Harris's *The End of Faith*, Daniel Dennett's *Breaking the Spell*, Richard Dawkins's *The God Delusion*, and Christopher Hitchens's *God Is Not Great*. If the uproar is any guide, these books evidently hit a nerve – and not just by their robust opposition to religion, which has lost the protective carapace of the respect which believers could once demand merely because they believed (a most odd situation, that, and one we are well rid of, given that there is nothing intrinsically respectable about believing old myths), but because they really do show that the emperor has not a stitch of clothing on his back.

In response to these powerful trumpet blasts, a new genre of religious apologetic has appeared, aimed at rebutting the atheist arguments and defending the faith. Here follow some remarks on contributions to each side of this battle of the books.

I take Hitchens's enjoyable and swingeing *God Is Not Great* first. A common charge levelled by religious apologists against their critics is that the latter do not understand the enticements of religion from within. As in so many other ways, they meet their match in Hitchens. He was brought up as a Christian in a family of partly Jewish extraction, and well understands the throat-catching beauty of language in the King James version, the moral stature of such figures as Martin Luther King, and the point of Marx's analysis of the role played by religion in the lives of the oppressed. But none of these things disguises, still less excuses, the false and too often wicked pretensions of religion as it infects history and the present. Hitchens addresses them one by one.

He begins by demolishing the metaphysical claim that the universe contains any supernatural agency or agencies, for once this is done and religions are seen for what they are, namely man-made constructions whose original point was to supply the ignorance of mankind's pre-scientific infancy, the main point can be tackled, which is to expose religion's many false-hoods and dangers. Hitchens charges that religion's foundational documents are fabrications, and that such usefulness as it might once have had to mankind lies well in the past, since when it has been a persistent balk to science and enquiry, and an enemy to freedom of speech and thought as well as to individual liberty. He charges that it sustains itself on lies and fears, that it has not only been the promoter of ignorance, guilt, sexual repression, torture, murder, hatred and violent fanaticism, but is the accomplice of slavery, genocide, racism and tyranny – and remains so.

None of these charges is deniable, and some of the main bureaucracies of religion have admitted the fact: witness the 'apologies' issued by the late Pope for the manifold sins and wickednesses of his Church throughout its history. In light of the remark that 'by their fruits we shall know them' this is telling. Hitchens attacks those turpitudes, and scarcely needs to answer the putative counter-argument that there would be no great works of art and architec-ture without religion. Of course there would: they are the product of humanity's creative urge, and any excuse would evoke them. (In any case: is the apologist's claim that burnings at the stake, witch-hunts, child-molestation, wars and mass exterminations, are an acceptable price for multiply iterated paintings of the Madonna, cathedrals, and plainsong?)

Hitchens also answers the canard that the secular tyrannies of fascism and communism have as bad a record as religion. One way of countering it is to observe that Torquemada's Catholicism, Talibanism, Nazism and Stalinism all share the same character: they are monolithic ideologies that coerce subservience to an ideal identified by those in power (the priesthood, the Party); and even display such similarities as enforced credos, the concept of thought-crime, and saints embalmed in mausoleums. Hitchens does not put the point in quite this way, articulating it instead, in closely similar terms, of their comparable totalitarian structure. He notes the similarity of outward forms, adds the details that apologists like to forget – for example, Hitler's religious sentiments, Stalin's education in a seminary – and reminds us that absolute monarchy was underpinned by the doctrine of the divine right of kings.

And how did the religions respond to the twentieth century's secular tyrannies, given their 'own

record of succumbing to, and promulgating, dicta-
torships on earth and absolute control in the life to
come', as Hitchens pointedly asks? Well: Pope Pius XI
described Mussolini as 'a man sent by providence'; a
1930s slogan of the Catholic right in France was 'meil-
leur Hitler que Blum'; almost all German Catholics
agreed with the tenor of this sentiment as applied
to their own country; and so one could go dispir-
itingly on. Hitchens points out too that another of
the aggressor tyrannies of the mid-century even had a
god as head of state: viz. Japan.

It is hard sometimes not to be withering about the
absurdities and evils of religion, and Hitchens is not
one to mince words. But his book is not a rant, any
more than a report of the crimes of the Inquisition or
Pol Pot would count as one. It accumulates a devas-
tating case, and only the most determined refusal to
concede to reason could allow a defender of religion
to come away from reading the book without very
big questions to answer.

Hitchens ends by calling for a 'new Enlightenment',
premised on the idea that the proper study of
mankind is man and woman. The unfettered pursuit
of science, the study of literature and poetry, and a
generous attitude to relations between people – all
of this now being within the reach of humankind for

the first time – is the true basis for achievement of the good, and Hitchens urges it. Not, he concedes, that achieving it will be easy or quick: but it is possible. The obvious first required step is liberation from religion.

Now let us contrast Hitchens's contribution to a book by physicist turned vicar, John Polkinghorne, and his assistant Nicholas Beale, optimistically entitled *Questions of Truth* (Westminster, John Knox Press).

Polkinghorne's former student Beale runs a website on behalf of his mentor, on which questions about religion, and the relation of religion to science, are posted and answered. The book is a compilation of fifty-one of these website questions with Beale's and sometimes Polkinghorne's answers. The questions range over creation, the existence of evil, evolution, intelligent design, and most of the other familiar debating points, plus 'How does the death of Jesus save the world?', 'Why believe Jesus rose from the dead?' and 'How much do you need to believe to be a Christian?'

Since these latter questions premise subscription to the faith already, I shall focus just on the various questions that touch on the relation of science and religion, because the interest attaching to Polkinghorne is, as noted, that he is a physicist who became a Church of England vicar, which makes people think that he has a special line into the science-religion question. Were he a vicar who gave up the Church of England to become a physicist he would not be regarded as anything other than sensible; but this is how the world wags.

It is needless to itemise the questions and their answers, because the former are the usual and familiar ones, and the answers given are familiar too. In brief, they come down to the tired old three: god-of-the-gaps, argument-to-the-best-explanation, and 'religion and science both seek the truth but in different domains'. There is no consciousness on the part of the authors of the inconsistency here: if the last answer is true, the first two are unnecessary; if either or both the first two are necessary, the third is false.

And of course Beale-Polkinghorne milk the tendentious version of the Anthropic Principle which has it that the constants of nature are fine-tuned in order that we can exist.

The gaps-god and best explanation strategies (which both come down to 'we don't know the answer so let's say Fred did it') can be left aside; undergraduates cut their teeth on refuting them. The 'non-overlapping magisteria' point, as it is now customarily called after

Stephen Jay Gould's coining of the expression, could likewise be left aside; religions make far too many claims about the origin and nature of the world and everything in it not to be in direct conflict with science over large tracts of explanation; but I will return to this in a moment because by it hangs a tale.

As for the Anthropic Principle: well, it passes belief that it can still be trotted out in this guise. The argument that the universe exists for the express purpose of making the existence of humans possible has long since been debunked, and it is discreditable of anyone, Beale-Polkinghorne included, to try to pass it off on the unsuspecting. In case anyone needs reminding, the point can be illustrated as follows: I would not be writing this on a laptop if computers had not been invented, but this does not prove that computers were invented so that I could write this.

So let us return to the 'non-overlapping magisteria' point, the 'truth but in different domains' manoeuvre, and dwell on it for moment. To get this to work you have to cherry-pick which bits of scripture and dogma are to be taken as symbolic and which as literally true – so: Genesis is symbolic, the resurrection of Jesus literally true – the chief criterion being convenience, with the resurrection as a bit of necessary dogma whose violations of biological laws you just have to accept, which it is easier to do if you do not think too hard about it. But you only apply the cherry-picking and reinterpreting to the religious sources; science is not so easy to treat in this way. The rule appears to be that where science and religion directly conflict – about the origin of the universe, let us say – the religious tale (Genesis) gets turned into symbol, thus sidestepping the possibility of direct and testable confrontation. And indeed there is no possible test of religious claims; again conveniently, 'God will not be tested'. Moreover, as Beale-Polkinghorne exquisitely show, they can by this technique of evasion, rewriting, special-pleading, Jesuitry and speciousness, provide a religion-consistent answer to every question and every objection: which reminds one of Popper's telling observation that a theory that is consistent with everything explains nothing.

Thus in short, on the religious side of things you make up truth as you go along, by interpreting and reinterpreting scripture to suit your needs and to avoid refutation by confrontation with plain fact; and by this means Beale-Polkinghorne can claim that both science and religion seek truth. I would call this dishonest if I did not think it is in fact delusional, which – since a kind of lunatic sincerity is involved – it rather palpably must be.

It happens that 'lunatic' is an appropriate term here, for the painful experience of wading through this book gave me an epiphany: that religious faith is extremely similar to the kind of conspiracy theory that sufferers from paranoid delusions can hold: both the paranoid and the faithful see a purposive hand in everything, plotting and controlling and guiding – and interpret all their experience accordingly.

I found the Beale-Polkinghorne explanation of natural evil (childhood cancers, tsunamis and earthquakes that drown or crush tens of thousands, and other marks of benign providence) bizarre, though it is novel. They say that the deity allows natural evils to happen because 'he' has given creation 'freedom to be and to make itself' – thus imputing free will to 'creation' to explain natural evil in the same way as moral evil is imputed to the free will of humans. That represents an heroic contribution to theology, even more so than the one offered by theologian Keith Ward, whom I debated on the subject of natural evil in the pages of *Prospect* magazine following the tsunami that killed one hundred thousand people in Thailand. Ward's eventual view, after being manoeuvred into a corner, was: that the deity is not omnipotent, and cannot stop things like tsunamis happening. At least this exonerates a deity from making them happen, or fashioning a world in which they happen, with arbitrary mass murder as the result for which the deity in question is therefore responsible. But it takes away the most interesting of any putative deity's characteristics, making it more like an extra-terrestrial of limited capacities.

And of course Beale-Polkinghorne – to return to them – have to be mind-brain dualists (see their chapter on this, in which their dualism is described in their own version of theological Nuspeak as 'dual aspect monism' in which 'mind and brain are not identical' while yet being *one thing* – work that one out!) in order for them to keep a place for the concept of 'soul', itself explained in a cloud of fudge by analogy with piano and the music played on it: I quote, '…layers…indeterminism…er…Penrose… chaos theory…quantum mechanics…er…all rather complicated…'

Indeed. What is not complicated, though, is the scandal that the Royal Society allowed its premises to be used for the launch of this book. The accompanying publicity material had in the small print the statement, 'This book is being launched at (not by) the Royal Society…' Indeed again. No doubt the Royal Society required this disclaimer to be entered somewhere, having reluctantly and uncomfortably felt that it had to give one of its Fellows (Polkinghorne was made one before becoming a vicar) use of its facilities because he asked. Of course the point is that Beale-Polkinghorne and their religious publishers wish to get as much of the respectability of the Royal Society rubbed off on them as they can. This is the strategy adopted by the Templeton Foundation too, of sidling up to proper scientists and scientific establishments and getting their religious fingers onto respectable coat-sleeves in the hope of furthering their agenda – which, to repeat what must endlessly be repeated in these circumstances, is to have the superstitious lucubrations of illiterate goatherds who lived several thousand years ago given the same credibility as contemporary scientific research.

In my view Polkinghorne dishonoured the Royal Society by exploiting his Fellowship to publicise this pamphlet on its precincts. The Royal Society should perhaps insist that, as it is one of the world's principal institutions serving science, and as there are thousands of other places where theology and religion are the staple and main point (churches, church halls, seminaries), there will be no more special pleading for and insinuation of religion by religious apologists within its doors.

Finally, it is worth recurring to the Intelligent Design debate again, given the vigorous efforts made by its lobby in the United States, its creeping encroachment into Britain, and the fact that it is a doctrine of Islam – and to do so through a look at a book by academic Steve Fuller called *Dissent over Descent* (2008).

I shall not devote time to detailed rebuttals of the arguments in Fuller's chapters entitled, 'Is there a middle ground between creation and evolution?' and 'Is intelligent design any less scientific than evolution?', because once one has tackled the premises on which their arguments rely, that effort is rendered unnecessary. As follows.

Fuller describes Intelligent Design (ID) theory as the project of establishing 'by the usual scientific appeals to reason and evidence' that the world and life in it were purposefully designed by an intelligent agency competent to the task of creating a universe. Call this Point 1.

Fuller claims that ID is 'behind the scientific revolution that has been under way in the West since the seventeenth century' because the motivating belief behind scientific enquiry is that 'nature is so constructed' that it can be understood because – as St Augustine taught us – man is made in the image of God and is therefore capable of understanding the universe. Call this Point 2.

Fuller claims that there is no such thing as a 'scientific consensus' anyway, and that it is false that evolutionary theory is the cumulative result of progress in scientific enquiry. Call this Point 3.

Fuller claims that science results from religion, that 'no plausible alternative has yet been offered to justify the pursuit of science as a search for the ultimate systematic understanding of reality' other than belief in a divine personal creator, and that 'atheism has done precious little for science'. Call this Point 4.

On Point 1: no, ID theory is not a project that proceeds on 'the usual scientific appeals to reason and evidence'. It starts from a fixed conclusion, and looks for evidence to support it. Does it specify what would refute the fixed belief in a designing intelligence that is its starting point? Does it tell us what would count as a test of what it has already accepted in advance, before the search for allegedly-supportive evidence begins? It does not. Science, by contrast, hypothesises, tests, and revises or abandons hypotheses when the evidence goes against them. There is a whole universe of difference between true science and the effort of ID theorists and creationists to find useful propaganda among the facts and alleged facts to support its prior convictions.

Fuller knows Karl Popper's work, but seems to forget Popper's killer point, namely, a theory that explains everything explains nothing. ID is such a theory; everything is consistent with it, nothing disproves it. The idea that there is such a thing as a deity behaves logically as a contradiction does (unsurprisingly, because the idea is indeed contradictory: 'god is omnipotent; does that mean he can eat himself' &c): anything whatever follows from it.

On Point 2: from a thousand years before St Augustine, Thales and the Pre-Socratics, Plato, Aristotle, the Stoics and the Epicureans, were thinking in recognisably scientific and proto-scientific ways about the nature and functioning of the universe, on the assumption that human intelligence is competent to understand the workings of nature, which observation abundantly suggests are regular and ordered – it needs no gods to point out how spring returns after every winter, and the crops grow again as they did before, and so manifestly on. Not only did people emphatically not have to wait for St Augustine to discover that they could enquire thus, without invoking supernaturalistic beliefs of any sort, but it is indeed a mark of the thought of Thales and his successors that they did not start from such beliefs, but started their thinking from observation and reason. It was the revival of their independence of thought in the Renaissance and afterwards – the rediscovery of a non-theistic tradition of thought about the world – that represents a resumption of the scientific enterprise that had been crushed by religious dogma for a millennium, and which in the sixteenth and seventeenth centuries had a struggle to free itself from religion's iron opposition – witness for instance the church's denial of Copernican heliocentrism and the trial of Galileo: and the religious are still at it today – the ID theorists are the inheritors of Cardinal Bellarmine in refusing to accept what science discovers, as is the Vatican in its opposition to stem cell research for example. About the only thing that can explain Fuller's effort to re-run the argument that modern science is the kindly gift of sixteenth century religion (of the Inquisition, perhaps, in the intervals between killing people who did not believe that e.g. the sun stood still over Jericho?) is ignorance.

Now as to Point 3, about the alleged absence of a 'scientific consensus' and the 'mistake' of thinking that evolutionary theory is a success story of cumulative enquiry. The latter we can pass over briefly: let us allow the cumulative confirmation of evolutionary theory to speak for itself, thus merely mentioning Lyell's geology, Darwin's wide-ranging observations and studies, Mendel's peas, the combination of genetic theory and understanding of selection both natural and artificial, the fossil record, comparative anatomy and physiology, and a mass of observation, experiment and discovery, and simply ask: nothing cumulative and progressive about this, eh?

The 'consensus' point requires a bit more attention. Fuller's claim here is the open-a-gap technique; if scientists disagree about something, if there is no consensus among them, perhaps you can slip an alternative – a god or two? a bit of putative intelligent design? – into the gap. But Fuller really is in a muddle here. He says there is no scientific consensus (in general? or only on a case-by-case basis in regard to some cutting-edge, currently-researched problem?) but nevertheless that there is a 'scientific orthodoxy' which, if you do not sign up to it, excludes you from access to its structures – presumably, to jobs and funding in science. Well: scientists tend to be clever people so I suppose they are capable of managing to have an orthodoxy without a consensus, though to me that sounds like a contradiction. But let's accept it momentarily. Is the universal agreement among scientists about the periodic table, the predictive power of quantum theory, the methods of testing efficacy of pharmaceutical compounds, and so on for a million such things, a mark of 'orthodoxy' but not a fundamental 'consensus' about basics, methods, and the like? Or might it just be the case that the foundations of science are very secure, universally accepted, and the basis on which open questions, research and debate proceed, and in the light of which they make sense? No doubt ID proponents like to characterise the existence of as-yet unsolved problems in science, and the way research opens new questions for examination, as 'evidence' that science is in some sort of disarray and in need of appeal to deities to sort it out (here the argument seems to be: scientists debate, they research, they sometimes disagree – so there must be a god!). But here is where Fuller's argument again collapses. If science is impugnable in the way he alleges, then his describing 'ID science' as proper science – without consensus! with a constraining orthodoxy! – is likewise impugnable. Can he have it both ways?

As to Point 4: Let us not forget that for a person to acknowledge openly that he or she was non-religious at any point before the nineteenth century in Europe or America was at least to invite social exclusion, at worst to invite death. So everyone 'was religious'. The education, such as it was, for most people was religious education; children learned to read by reciting in rote from the Bible as the children in Pakistan's madhrassas today learn the Koran's suras by rote. Even we atheists say things like 'for god's sake!' and 'oh hell!' So when any historically derived idea not actually part of the dogma or scriptures of some religion is described as a 'religious' idea it might as informatively be described as a 'human idea' or 'a social idea'. In a chapter subtitle Fuller writes 'Consensus: The Extension of a Religious Idea to Science'. You see the technique: how easy it is to ascribe everything to a source in religion, because religion was historically the social element as water is the element in which fish live. Attributing anything other than specific doctrine to 'religion' is therefore vacuous.

This, though, is another mark of ignorance and historical short-sightedness. As the dominant religion of Europe and the world it conquered, Christianity imported large helpings of Greek philosophy to supply the deficiencies in its ethics and metaphysics, starting with the importation of Neoplatonism some centuries after the lifetime of Jesus when it was clear that the imminently expected end of the world had been postponed, and reaching high tide in the late medieval period with the patching of Aristotle into theology, effected by Aquinas and some of the Schoolmen. Many of the ideas that are often attributed to a religious source in the modern period are therefore secular, non-theistic borrowings from the

Greeks, tacked onto the incoherencies of faith, and rescued from that affiliation by the resumption of rational enquiry in the scientific revolution.

And what has atheism done for science? Well, let us see: it removed the risk of scientists being burned at the stake for controverting the divinely-revealed truth that 'the lord hath laid the foundations of the earth so that it shall not be moved for ever' (Psalm 102, beloved of Bellarmine in his efforts to silence the astronomers and philosophers of the era of Descartes). It removed the necessity of having to distort observations, facts, experimental results and observations, to fit with an antecedent doctrine as far from what observation and experiment revealed as one could possibly get. (Think about seeing the moons of Jupiter through a telescope in an age when the earth was – by order! – at the centre of the universe, and man and his man-made religion was the most important thing in it, with the Pope and the Office of the Inquisition daring you to think otherwise.) In short, it liberated the mind and enquiries of mankind. Decreasing religious hegemony and rapidly increasing scientific and technological knowledge have gone *pari passu* during the last four centuries, in mutually-reinforcing tandem: the less religion, the more science; the more science, the less religion. And this is a universal phenomenon (even in the USA; see the Pew polls on the decline of religion even there).

Here I have commented only on some of the premises of Fuller's book. The demerits of ID theory itself are so woeful as almost to be funny. In this world of ours – with nature, for all its wonders and beauties otherwise, also showing so much failed experiment, so much repetition and haphazard variety of endeavour to meet the challenge of passing on genes – to claim the existence and activity of a supernatural designer would be a sort of blasphemy on the latter, if it existed. All this is well-enough known not to require the effort of iteration; nor does the overwhelming security of evolutionary theory in biology require defence. It is only because of the persistence of those who are not satisfied to have religious beliefs but want others to have them too, and therefore strive to persuade others of their beliefs, that it is necessary to have to debate again what should really by now be in the dustbin of history along with witches and fairies and flat earth theories.

6

The Good Life

T HE QUARREL BETWEEN religion and its opponents in contemporary society is a noisy one,
as the foregoing pages have again attested. The
success of Richard Dawkins's *The God Delusion* and
other atheist books has raised the stakes between
those who think religion is an important part of
life, and those who see it as a hindrance to progress
and truth. The different faiths, for their part, have
become increasingly assertive in recent years, even
to the extent of taking up arms and committing
murder in the name of their various gods, prophets
and sanctities.

One of the most significant aspects of the religion
quarrel concerns morality. Religious people think
that morals are undermined if they are not based on a
belief in a deity. The more austere among them think
that the pursuit of pleasure and the desire for possessions have promoted selfishness and frivolity at the
expense of moral principle: 'the good life' has, they
say, supplanted 'living a life of goodness'.

Is this true? Is 'the good life' incompatible with a good life? Most people want pleasure, achievement and material comfort in their lives, and yet also want to live a morally good life too. On the face of it there seems little reason why these ambitions should be inconsistent. And yet for most of history the prevailing view, based on religion, has been that 'the good life' cannot be morally good, on the grounds that pleasure and the desire for material possessions undermine one's moral fibre, and make one vulnerable to temptation. This view is making a comeback with the resurgence of the faiths, not least among the more conservative groups of Muslims and Christian evangelicals.

As it happens, people who seek pleasure and material comforts have often enough given religious moralists cause for concern. Think of Roman banquets, Renaissance feasts, Restoration comedies and Regency excesses, and the difference between the experience thus connoted and the moral experience chosen by monks, Puritans, and sober-faced Sunday-observing Victorians. Note the antagonists: they are not the possessors of a particular moral outlook and, say, Holocaust-perpetrating Nazis, whom it is not the special task of religion to oppose, for every right-minded person, religious or not, opposes them. It is the far more trivial opposition between the tipsy fornicator and the po-faced preacher. But underlying the contrast here is an interesting and more serious difference of view about the nature of human beings, and even about the nature of goodness itself.

For most of history people believed that human beings are quite different from the rest of nature because they possess reason and language. They unquestioningly assumed that humanity was created by a deity, who gave each individual an immortal soul. In medieval times humanity was seen as the central point between earth and heaven, standing at the pivot of the Great Chain of Being which extended from the lowliest worm to the deity itself.

Given this view, it is no surprise that what was regarded as good was whatever would save man from his beastly physical nature and its appetites, in order to prepare him for the purely spiritual felicity of life after death. Pleasures and possessions were therefore dangerous, because they distracted his attention from his heavenly goal.

There is a great difference between this view and one that sees humanity as part of nature. This was what the ancient Greeks thought. They praised friendship, the quest for knowledge, and the appreciation of beauty, as the greatest human pleasures. The focus of their attention was this world and its benefits, and they debated intelligently about how to make the most of them.

The central part of their enjoyment of this-worldly pleasures was of course not congenial to religious minds, so it had to wait for the Renaissance to be rediscovered. During the long centuries of the Church's dominion over hearts and minds (from the fourth century to the fifteenth century CE) people were taught that the world is a vale of tears, a place of traps set by the devil, of trial, suffering and woe. This outlook was expressed in sermons, *contemptus mundi* tracts, murals and altar-pieces depicting the agonies of punishment for sin. It was also reflected in the architecture of Gothic churches, whose soaring towers rose into the heavens above the dirt and decay of the physical world below.

The leading Renaissance minds took a very different view from this. They were so conscious of the contrast that one of their earliest luminaries, Petrarch, coined the term 'Middle Ages' to describe what he saw as the dark period between the bright civilisation of classical antiquity and the renewed joy that he and his contemporaries took in art, nature, music, poetry, love, and all things human.

The Renaissance thinkers argued that man is a part of nature, and that it is natural to celebrate what pleases the five senses – colours and tastes, scents and sensations, music and the lover's touch. Modern science confirms this Renaissance intuition. We know from biology and genetics how much we are part of nature, and how much all the things that were once thought to distinguish humankind from other animals is in fact widely shared by them. The first full realisation of this truth came with Darwin, and has since been overwhelmingly attested from ten thousand different proofs. It tells us that the range of this-worldly things people find to appreciate in life, and the things that give them pleasure and satisfaction, are as natural to them as the desire for food and drink.

This is why there is nothing wrong with the pleasures and possessions of 'the good life'; they are what people naturally seek and even need. Of course it must be added that there is nothing wrong with them provided that they are not enjoyed at the expense of someone else, and so long as the business of acquiring them does not become an obsession or end in itself. Trampling on others to get ahead, and becoming obsessed with money rather than the good things that it can buy, are hardly the stuff either of 'the good life' or a life of goodness.

Contrary to the religious anxiety about 'the good life', then, it is arguable that pleasures and possessions not only make life enjoyable, but they make other positive things possible too. The better things are in one's own life, the more good one can do to other people. Among the best things anyone can have are successful relationships with friends, family and community. That is quite different from the mistaken picture of 'the good life' as something selfish and even debauched. If this is what 'the good life' is, it would soon become miserable, because debauched pleasures are quickly exhausted, and pursuing them is unlikely to result in good relationships with others.

Here then is a way of deciding between the religious and non-religious view of morality. The rich tradition of thought stemming from ancient Greece teaches that there is no conflict between 'the good life' and a life that is morally good. The opposite view disagrees with this because it says that mankind should avoid being too much part of nature. The Greek view, like modern science, recognises that we are natural beings – part of nature, part of its continuum, related to it, dependent on it, and now responsible for it. Some of the religions have lately abandoned their earlier long-standing view that because humans are essentially supernatural (invested with immortal souls) and that nature was 'given' to them to exploit, they have no duty to be ecologically responsible; and this they have done in order to scramble aboard the environmental bandwagon which their original views were in danger of forcing them to miss. But in making this change to doctrine they are challenged with uncomfortable consequences they have yet to face.

Take just one example: is the celibacy of the Catholic priesthood consistent with the nature of humans as sexual and reproductive beings? To be fully human is to acknowledge and respond to that fact. In effect therefore Catholicism requires priests to distort themselves into denying and suppressing their human nature. We know the cost of such distortion in, for example, child sex abuse. But Catholic doctrine on sex impinges on all its votaries; every Catholic must be a sexually truncated being, and if not then they must be promiscuously reproductive even at the expense of their own and their (too many) offsprings' welfare. In sum Catholic teaching on sex, illustrative of its view of humanity's nature, is a kind of madness, dispassionately viewed; and most lay Catholics (and many ordained ones) in practice do not, because they cannot, go along with it. And so the net effect of the teaching is hypocrisy and a great deal of unnecessary psychological pain. Which is the good and well-lived life here: the distortion, denial and truncation, the enslavement to too much childbirth and too many children, or the hypocrisy and psychological pain of answering nature in defiance of Catholic moral teaching on sex? Whichever way you look at it, Catholic moral teaching on sex is a ghastly mess.

That is just one example from just one sect of just one religion, and one could multiply examples endlessly of the conflict of religion with human nature. This is not to say that human nature is good because natural: far from it: for many aspects of it, such as aggression and the appetites including sex, require government in the interests of that other great fact of humanness, namely its essential sociality. But that government is better effected along the grain of human nature than across it. To channel rather than to block the energies of human nature, to understand and better employ rather than to chastise and forbid them, would surely be the best way to manage most of those energies. This is what a society's negotiation with itself about law and ethics addresses, and it has to do so in an evolving and responsive way over time. The frozen imposition of an antique morality, like the frozen imposition of an antique view of the world, is harmful and becomes more so as time and history proceed. Witness the conflict between Islam and the modern world: by its nature unable to adapt, reinterpret and reinvent itself, Islam is in the process of colliding messily with modernity, and threatening to do a lot of damage to everyone else in the process.

We already have the basis of a universal ethics by which humanity, in all its variety and tumult, can rub along with itself: the framework of human rights.[4] As these words were written the Organisation of Islamic Conferences (OIC) was making every effort at the United Nations Human Rights Council in Geneva to change the Universal Declaration of Human Rights to conform with its own Islamic version of human rights, which for example does not accord the same rights to women as men, and which seeks to criminalise 'defamation of religion' (which means: criticism of or opposition to religion). If an example were needed of how religion works tirelessly to drag the world backwards, this is a particularly striking one. It is all the more troubling in light of the fact that the single most important advance that the world now needs is the full enfranchisement of women everywhere, something against which Islam strives.

The sources of a full, rich, deep understanding of human nature lie across the whole range of human

---

4   I discuss humanistic ethics and their relation to thinking about human rights in *The Choice of Hercules* (2008).

endeavour, from the arts to the sciences. Biology, ethology, anthropology and palaeoanthropology, sociology, psychology, literature, philosophy, and the study of history, all make their contributions to the great endeavour of human self-understanding that goes hand-in-hand with humanity's endeavour to learn more about the surrounding universe of nature also. The present quarrel between religious and non-religious attitudes towards these coupled endeavours marks a further chapter, and perhaps a decisive one, in the story of mankind's effort to escape the lingering negative aspects of its past in search of a future. In the last three or four centuries of Western history that effort, inch by painful inch, has produced much that promises much: but the promise has still to be fulfilled. One contribution towards that end is to keep insisting on the arguments and considerations offered in the foregoing pages, and others like them, in the hope of liberating more and more of mankind from the thrall which would deny that promise, and which would thereby keep Prometheus bound to his rock for ever. Our watchword must therefore always and insistently be: let us strive to set Prometheus free.